TRUNK CALLS

Christian Poems for Today

by

Johnny McCarthy

CAMPUS PUBLISHING

ISBN 1 873223 30 7

Typesetting by Wendy Commins
Printed and bound by Colour Books Ltd.

Published by
Campus Publishing
26 Tirellan Heights
Galway
Ireland

Contents

DEDICATION

*With love and gratitude to my Mother
and also to my Father
and my Brothers and Sisters and Friends*

Foreword

by

Anne Jennings

The first time I heard Johnny McCarthy's poetry was at a friend's house in Galway one night.

There were about fifty of us there. We had been praying for a while together and, during the course of a rather formal setting, Johnny read one of his poems.

It was a kind of "Story-prayer" effort, expressed in the most informal way. The message was plain and simple: change your ways or else! But the humour and relaxed tone of the poem evoked a very positive response.

This is how Johnny does it—simple, clear and straight to the point. That's why they go down very well with a lot of young people I meet in my work as a teacher. There's no threat, no fear, no push—just a nice way of saying that God loves you in a variety of ways.

They are a treat to read because you don't have to ponder for ages on their meaning. And above all, they are deep and honest reflections of a rather long and difficult faith journey. There's at least one poem to match your present faith stage, whatever that is.

I am certain that these poems will enlighten you and allow you to see yourself really there.

When I read Johnny's poetry I feel that Jesus is not only divine but a real human being, just like any of us. And in today's world, we must be able to relate to Jesus as just that.

Carriage Ride

My wallet is bare
My head is bad
The horse's tail is wagging
in my eye
I feel so bad I think
I'll die

Tourists asking about the ride
and who are you
Clippety clop goes the horses' shoe

Where was I last night
Hope I did not give
anyone a fright
Wonder if I had a good time
drinking that expensive wine

Clippety clop nearly fell off
Wake up Johnnie you're
not in bed
Make sure the reins
are on the horse's head

Round this blooming
park again
Who said it was great
living in sin

A Life Anew

When you have
nowhere to go
and suicide smiles
and God seems like He is
a million miles away

You know He is there
yet you have no belief
in prayer

What do you do
Who do you turn to
King alcohol or king dope
or perhaps a gambling spree

You think God must
be worth a try
Ain't nothing else gonna
stop you getting high
Your emotions are wrecked
and outa shape
something like an unbaked cake

You pray and say
God You're not there
but please help anyhow

Can't stop crying
Can't stop lying
Can't help my unbelief

I want to be good
and so I should
But king alcohol has me beat

If You're there
You will hear my prayer
and turn my life around

No more hangovers
and my memory gone
or crying in my sleep

No more money down the drain
No more saying sorry
and hiding my shame

Then slowly you see
your life starting to change
and slowly you come to believe

that the God
you once rejected
had gently sowed His seed

Your life now
is a beautiful creation
Thanks to the Lord and
His merciful salvation

He never forgot you
or let you down
although you had acted
like a foolish clown

If you don't believe
ask and you will receive
the grace of faith
and trust in God
and gifts He will
give to you

You will be happy
patient and kind
and you will have
lots of courage too

Jesus Christ is
not a messer
He just simply
loves you.

With Your Help Lord

Lord we know you are good
at English and great at Philosophy too
How about some inspiration
that will see us through the exams

Lord throw the devil out the door
he is such an awful bore
Pour some holy water
on his head
It might cool him down
He is always talking nonsense
the silly clown

Our prayer lives are up and down
like a big see-saw
Please give us the strength
to get it right
We know it will
do us good

Help us too with
the people we meet
Help us greet them nicely
when we meet them on the street

Thank you Lord for everything
especially all our friends
Thank you for rising
from the dead
One day we hope to too.

Your promise is your word
We know you are always right
Thank you Lord
for each beautiful night.

Spring '89

Did you ever wonder if there's a God at all
Is he big or is he small
I wonder why the birds fly
while nature around me buds
like the cabbage plant
or the Brussels sprout
I wonder if Solomon had the gout
Is responsibility the key
to be happy in reality?

Heartache

When it comes to women
a man should be mysterious
and distant
Get close and they will
throttle you
Then you are left feeling
a mysterious distant fool

Yet foolishness is good for humility
It takes one away
from any feeling of nobility

I want her in my arms
I want to use all my charms
I want to whisper sweet
things in her ear

What will she say
this beauty of God
eyes dancing in her head
eyes of love and face serene
What would I not do
for this beauty queen

Don't know if my charms
will win her into my arms
Don't know if my God will
send me dismay
as I dream of love
for this man of clay

What will I do
with this maddening emotion
Should I let it sink
into the ocean
Will I ask her
then I'll know
whether it's sink or swim
It's up to God you know.

The Answer

Well Lord you sent me dismay
I'm sorry to say
What do you want
of me anyway

Are you asleep
or are You awake
If I could catch you
I would give you a shake

Thanks a lot
for this little trial
It's like dipping my toe
in burning oil

Yourself and St Peter
should go and have some tea
When you get back
then you will see
what your will for me is to to be

Whether it's a wife, a bishop
or a hermit on a hill
It's up to you
and Your mighty will

Lord don't forget where I am
I always hope to be your man

Hurts

Lord you're some cookie
You heal me with hurt
You stick my head in the dirt

Here are my troubles
Here are my woes
Please Lord bless my foes

I'm happy doing Your will
but sometimes I think I lack
the skill to be your disciple

I know it's not skill that's needed
Still I sometimes forget that

Lord wait for me
I'm going down the road with You
You see

Let me feel Your joy
Let me experience your love
Fill me with your spirit
from head to toe

Let me vibrate with life
at its best
for it is only in you Lord
I will find true rest

Acceptance

When we are feeling good
and things are going fine
It's easy to believe in God
and to give Him lots of time

But when life is dull
and nothing's going right
and we cannot see the stars
because of the cloudy night

This is the time
to persevere in prayer
This is the time to say Lord
we are going to hang in there

We will accept the things
we cannot change
We will change the things we can
Give us the wisdom to seek You
in gentle contemplation

Lord rid us of our fears
Make our souls spotless and clear
for you are the healer
You fill us with life
Your breath is fire Lord
always in control

Fill us Lord make us whole
for Thine is the Kingdom
the Power and the Glory
now and forever

Do It

What is motivation
Is it anticipation of a life to come
Is it something you buy
Is it something that will make you high
Where do you find it
Is it under a rock
Do you get it like
an electric shock

Is it in satisfaction or
is it a distraction or
is it a life of constant action

Where are you motivation
Have you just pulled out
of Galway station

Come back again
shining and blue
and help a poor soul
live his life true

God Is The Good Samaritan

Jesus is the master and to us
His life He gave
Jesus is the bridge
and through Him we cross
into paradise where we will meet
the Boss

The Boss is God the Father
This world He did make
He made it all so beautiful
you can be sure it's not a fake

The spirit brings us life
an everlasting one at that
God is so wonderful
that He never hangs his hat
or takes a rest
or says go away
when we are being a pest

A little note on faithfulness
It's easy to attain
when we open our hearts
to Mary
our prayer is heard quite plain

God is the good Samaritan
Jesus is His son
The Holy Spirit is the helper
and faithful to them
we should be
if we want to see the Kingdom
God has prepared
for you and me

Stuck On The Train

Lord I'm nearly broke
and all alone
Where can I reach You
by telephone

What's Your number
I will give You a call
and then proceed to tell
You all the things that
are bothering me

Ding ding ding Johnny
What's bothering you

Well Lord the exams are looming
I have other things
for doing
no study done yet

My prayer life is in a state
My head is going
at an awful rate
just gotta unwind

The train is stopped
in the middle of nowhere
The cows are chewing grass outside
They sure ain't worried
about the devil

I'm staying out too late at night
When I go to bed
the stars are bright
Maybe I should go
to bed early

I have been taking too
much vitamin B
Now I can't sleep properly
at all you see

Well Lord these are
my troubles
I'm sure there is more
but I don't want to be a bore

You did not forget my number
thanks a lot for the call
when I get to heaven
then we will have a ball
Catch you later Lord
thanks for ringing . . . *Ding*

Reality

I wish I was in the Bahamas
getting me some sun
I wish I had a yacht
to sail the seven seas
I wish I had a girlfriend
to sit upon my knees

I wish I had a house
with a swimming pool in it
I wish I had a cooker
with a built-in mighty chef
I wish I had a dog
that wasn't kinda deaf

I wish I was a popstar
singing tunes of love
I wish I was in heaven
hanging out with the man above

I wish I was a ballet dancer
tiptoeing gently
I wish I was a hermit
living in harmony

I wish I had a million
and I would give it all away
to some poor
undernourished creature
who would then have his way

What are wishes anyhow
They are projections
and not living in the now

Reality is painful
and God's plan is hard to suss
But in finding out His will
happiness comes to us

Doubt

Doubt in my head
Doubt in my bones
Can't reach God
on my Walkman earphones

Feeling lost about what to do
Should I join the navy
and see the world
Become a farmer minding sheep
be a chimney cleaner
cleaning flues
or a veterinary surgeon curing hoose

How about a social worker in Calcutta
or a secretary in Skibbereen
or perhaps I'll settle down
with a very rich beauty queen

Dear Lord I'm fed up praying
fed up saying Thank You for
all the good things in my
life

Why I'm like this I don't know
Just can't seem to let the
spirit flow
drifting in and out of prayer
even waking up with the odd nightmare

God You're so good and awful nice
and I'm not being a bit polite
Hold on and I'll apologise
If I could only see you
I would not criticise

I would be on my knees
saying Thank You God and
Hallelu
I'll do whatever You tell me to

Lord are all people this
blind or is it just me
Pity you don't have a channel
on the TV

Anyway Lord feel better now
Life sure is fun
And with Your help we will
beat the devil at his game
and go to heaven just the same

Pathfinder

We got angels on the bonnet
We got God on our side
We got four wheels driving us
and we got peace of mind

The devil tried to get us
but he went and missed
cause the good Lord has us
in His mighty fist

There is Blessed Mary
and her sweetness we cannot hide
She consoles us in our troubles
and listens to our woes
She tells everything to Jesus
and makes friends of our foes

She leads the fighters
in the Book of Revelation
This lady clothed with the sun
draws us to Jesus our salvation

We know the outcome to this war
for woman she will win
for our good God
created her free from the stain of sin

We will reign with her in heaven
and shine her crown of gold
Hail Mary full of grace
Your messages will unfold

Roses

Life's not a bed of roses
and roses smell quite sweet
They are also very painful
when they stick into your feet

Who knows the mind of God
Who knows His gentle caress
Who knows the fragrance
of the painful rose
smelling sweetly as it goes
into the bosom of your
very soul

The Lord says
Pick up your cross and
follow me
I will lead you to liberty
Before the wage there comes the work
Before the calm the storm of sea
Before peace Gethsemane

Look unto me
for all things
Be aware of the crown
that awaits you
in a mansion made of gold
Think of the life given you
its secrets to unfold

Leave the past behind you
Look Me full in the face
and I will lead you to heaven
where you will attain
the fullness of your grace

Busy

There is rain coming down
on your briefcase
through the hole in your umbrella
Troubles weigh you down and
you are rushing for the train

Stop and say
What is this world about
Where is the happy plane
Where is the God of Jacob
Has He left me in the lurch
How come I don't see Him
every time I go to church

Where are the scented flowers
and the happy life of man
Where is the serenity promised us
by God's almighty plan

Do we search under rocks of
gold
When the answer stares us in
the eye
Perhaps our vision is clouded
by dreams towering high

Your rock of gold is your
life created specially for you
Do not waste a moment
unhappy or with a frown
Live your life today
happy as a clown

Don't let the devil catch you
with thoughts of idle glee
for none of this will bring you
any serenity

I know the answer to your quest
It's fill your life with love
and happiness will be given you
from the hands of God above

A Talk

God and me
we went for a drive
out by Salthill
and down to the sea

Well I started talking
and said I'm fed up and angry
Things are not going my way
When I ask you what's wrong
You ain't got nothing to say

Johnny I am the Lord listen to me
You're going round like
I'm not there

What do you think
Is it that I don't care
I know every movement
you have ever made
I have watched you
asleep in your bed

Your trust my son
is way outa line
Your ego is hungry
not humble and mine

Not to worry
Let's try again
No man yet
has kept outa sin

Remember St Peter
after hearing the cock
Yet it was on this
same man that I
built my rock

So if you fall
don't run away
Just get back up again
and say

Lord that ould divil
will not get me down
I repent of my doubts
and foolish ways
Please be with me
every moment today

In Times Of Trouble

I will bless the Lord
at all times
His praise always on my lips
even when discouraged
and when enthusiasm
is on the wane
I will call on the Lord
my God to protect me
with His flame

What should I care
if I fall into the deepest ocean
or have to cross the harshest sea
Somehow I know the good Lord
is there and He will wrap
His arms around me
and guide me with His strength
for in Him all things are possible
and in Him our souls shall rest

And though sometimes we doubt
when we are put to the test
never fear never mind

The Lord is good
The Lord is kind
He will win through and through
because He simply loves you

Prayer

Our Lord He prayed
on bended knee
Our Lord He prayed
and died to set us free

Prayer is timeless and eternal
like a heart that's always
beating
like a rainbow that never
ends

It's the majesty of the falling star
It's the torrent of the Amazon
It's the mountains that surround us
It's the air we breathe
It's the scent of heaven
It's longevity we will never understand
It's to practise the presence
of God in our lives
and to thank Him
for what He sends
for He knows best
and His love it never ends.

Everything

There is a man called Jesus Christ
and he loves this world you know
He knows every part of it
like a violinist knows his bow

He conducts His orchestra
with consuming ease
The richness of his music
will bring you to your knees

From a mother's womb
to Gethsemane
and on to that cross
on Calvary

From the Resurrection
to the hope He brings
to life hereafter
in desert springs

Lord you bring us
hope and happiness
You bring this life
that we possess

You fill our souls
with the music of life
We are your creation
Thank You for Your Kingdom Lord
We await it in joyful anticipation

Mother

You dried us
when we were wet
You held us
when we were upset

You were there
when we cried
You were there
when we were hurt or in hospital
You were there
when we needed love
and you always
welcomed home the prodigal

You were there
to help us in our choice of life
You were there to advise us
if we needed a wife

You were always there for us
with words of hope and encouragement
Keep trying
God's will will be done
and you would throw in the odd word
and life
would seem like a lot of fun

And when sickness came
you always seemed
to pull through
but this time
it wasn't just another flu
This time it was cancer
and you had not long to live
You still did not worry
You still had a lot to give

Your faith came out
like a blossoming rose
with no fear of death
that long repose
You still encouraged us with words
Don't worry it's not so bad
This is life and it's sometimes sad
So be strong keep on living
Keep your faith
Keep on giving

Mother in your time of trial
the nurses and doctors
showered you with love
and the neighbours
were sent from God above

Ma we are sure
you are in heaven
with the Lord
and His Mother too
and we know that the angels
are singing merrily
with you

Mother from your friends
and relations
from your brothers and sister
and from Dad and the eight of us
Goodbye for a little while

It's Not Easy Sometimes

Battered bruised but not broken
like Christ on His cross
Wonder what He was feeling
when He said "Father
You're the Boss"

Sometimes in life
when the burdens are large
and you are feeling bad
you say to God
I've had enough
Don't want any more
of that blooming stuff

You know He's God
You don't know His will
You know His cross is
a perfect fit
that will get you to heaven
maybe right up to the top

So let's accept our crosses
and live joyfully
We will all be happy
in eternity

Fire and Brimstone

What good is fortune and fame
What good is a beautiful dame
What good is all the money in the world
if the love of God is not
unfurled on your humble existence

You can drive shiny cars
You can wine and dine
in the best bars

Your credit may be good
your washing machine brand new
your video the latest from Japan

You may dress in fashionable
clothes
Your skin might sparkle
from head to toe

You may go on holidays
to tropical isles
and come back home
with beautiful smiles

You may think of life
as a merry-go-round
with money in your pocket
and where good friends abound

You fools
Your eyes glimmer with gold
Your heads are a maze
of untold ambitions

Do you think of God
as a rational being
who can be bought
with a beauty queen

Do you see the old
forgotten and alone
Do you dream of the poor
the lonely the lame

Do you see
the children
who suffer life's blame

Do you try to help just a little bit
Do you try
to make the misfits fit

When you meet your maker
what will you say to Him
what will you say to Him
Will you sink
or will you swim
It's up to God
not your whim

Happenings

Lord I'm sure heaven
is a lovely place
with lots of things to do
like talking to my ancestors
or perhaps just visiting with You

Lord I know you were
here on earth 2000 years ago
Things have changed a lot
since then
I thought I would let You know

We have multi-channel TV
beamed in from outer space
We have every type of gadget
cluttering up the place

We have discos in the bars
and under-age drinkers

We have politicians
who talk about everything
from potholes to the national lottery
They even wanted to take
You out of the constitution
and replace you with some tomfoolery

We have star wars
and oil slicks
and billions spent
on the arms race

We have famines
and health cuts
Drug addiction is high
There is so much
pain in this world
that sometimes we want to cry

Lord there is one thing
that keeps us going
It's the hope we possess
that somehow You're in charge
of this wonderful mess

Worms

There is a worm crawling up
my back
I wonder what's his name
Is it influenza slipped disc or
something of the same

Is it the father who's in hospital
Is it the niece who's not too
good at school or is it
the young fella who's working
over in Blackpool

Lord these cares and troubles
weigh me down and I
cannot pray
for my mind is clogged with
the worries of this day

Listen Child tell Me your problems
I am right by your side
I am always with you
Death will not even take us apart
for I the Lord have you
always in My heart

Now Child listen well and listen
good
to what I have to say
How can I rid you of your
problems if you will not
give them away

Remember all things work unto
good for those who love
the Lord
When you do as I suggest
happiness will be your reward

Do not hang onto troubles
that will weigh you down
Hand them over to Me
without even a frown

Then go about your business
happy and with faith too
for I the Lord your God
just simply love you

Our God

The Lord is God of water schemes
car engines and bicycles too
The Lord is God of nuclear energy
secretaries and the zoo

Our God made the oceans and
the planes that cross them
as well
He made all things in heaven and
in hell

Our God made the stars the
sun and the moon He also
made each child that was ever
in a mother's womb

Jesus died and rose again
and when He stepped out of
that tomb
He showed us that He will
come back again
soon and very soon

God Is In Each One

It's easy being nice
and easy being sweet
when we see God
in the people we meet

If you saw Jesus
with his car
stuck in the flood
you would say

Hang on there
I will give you a tow
and pull you right out of
that blessed flow

If you saw Mary
stranded in her house
you would say

Come with me
I will give you a bed
a hot lemon as well
I will put on the electric
blanket and all will be swell

If you saw Joseph
fixing his front door
but the rain was so bad
he could not cope any more
you would say

Joseph and your family
Come stay with me
Don't worry about the cost
this treat's on me

If you saw Peter
with hungry sheep
in the rocks
you would help him
to feed his flock

The Lord is our shepherd
that's for sure
please Lord help us to give
to the poor the old
the lonely the sick

For it is in giving
we receive the grace
to live your message
of love

and then
when we meet
God above

He will say
Well done
good and faithful servant
Yours is the Kingdom of Heaven

Holy Spirit

This is what the Holy Spirit
means to me
It's a gentle breeze and
a howling wind
It is an eternal tree
that will not bend

It's a purpose-filled life
which brings faith in God
It's a freedom which shines
forth from our being
The Holy Spirit is not unseen

It's in tongues of fire
with unquenchable flames
Its radiance never wanes
Its richness can never be known
Its beauty never matched
Its eternity is in each one
with the Father and the Son

How to acquire this spirit
we ask
It's a simple but not an
easy task
Watch and pray
Sing out strong
Say yes Father we belong

Give us wisdom
Give us truth
Give us faith hope and love in You
and give us the knowledge to
discern what to do

Send your gifts that
we may enrich the world
Let us bring Jesus
to the hungry
and to the lame
who cry for Your name

Praise you Father
Praise you Jesus
Praise the Holy Spirit too
for You alone are our shepherd
and our lives belong to You

Apparition Time

Wisps of smoke curl
around the cross of Christ
on the hill of Podeo
in Medugorje

The nations are gathered
Cameras click
Candles flicker
People are praying
and singing songs of praise

Apparition time is near
A visionary shouts Kneel
The smoke billows in
silent adoration
It wafts through the crowd
as if in an act of purification

Peace is in the air
We feel her presence
Our hearts flutter
Our minds turn to the greatness
of God

Electric moments seemingly
never ending
Our Lady extends her arms
and prays

her message—
She is happy
with the youth of the world

Hope encouragement
Life everlasting

Mother Mary thanks
for being our friend
and for introducing us
to life without end

A Mháthair

I can almost
see her face
through the haze
of the shadowed moon

A purple cloak
surrounds her
as she sits
on the throne of grace

The mother of our God
loves us
Her kindness
knows no bounds

Did she not
watch Jesus
as He fell
to the ground

Her counsel is wisdom
Her touch is sure
Her love is gentle and pure
consoling and compassionate

Her eyes are
a gentle hue
burning bright
with love for me and you
Intercede for us
Mother Mary
Enrich our lives
we pray

Bring us closer
to Jesus
each and every day

The Eucharist

A priest home from Argentina
I listened to one day
What he said was
Go to Jesus in the Blessed Sacrament
He will teach you how to pray

The Lord waits for us in the Host
He is really there even if it's
snowing the Lord does not care

He waits for us with patience
He waits for us with love
He never gets tired of listening
to our problems or our cares
Even when we are angry
His temper never flares

Our Mother Mary also asks us
to spend time with her son
for the moments we spend in adoration
will help us to overcome
every kind of temptation

And when in the morning of our lives
our days are fruitfully done
Jesus will welcome us into his Kingdom
as His daughters or His sons

He will say
Nice to see you
Many conversations we have had
You never forgot me even though
some of your days were bad

My child you have loved much
Yours is the Kingdom of Heaven

Healing

Lord take our imaginations make them Yours
Lord take our lives make them Yours
Lord take our emotions make them whole
Fill us with Your Love
in body and in soul

Heal us in Your special way
So that our spirits
will not know decay

Lord let us not doubt Your
Holy Word
which brings knowledge of
everlasting life

Let it enrich us we pray
Let it deepen our faith
day by day

And as from the abyss
of Your heart
flows everlasting love

Let it burn
Let it glow
Let it show
in our faces
as we go
about our daily tasks

Sometimes

Sometimes when we make mistakes
and things are in a muddle—
You might have had one of those days
when you stepped into a puddle—

We can go to the Lord
and say to him
Lord this is an awful day
Come help me back
onto the right track
for I fear I'm being
led astray

The Lord will say
There is a power in prayer
that will free you from care
You won't give a damn
if you're in a jam
You won't give a hoot
if you have no loot

Pray to the saints
and my Mother too
They will be sure
to intercede for you
So how about a smile
or a happy grin
Life's great begin again

Bad days come
Bad days go
Why not let me run the show?
My name is Jesus
I'm the Son of God
I love you
you lucky sod

Christian Books from Campus

JUST A MOMENT
by Father Colm Kilcoyne

Father Colm Kilcoyne invites you to spare just a moment to consider many of today's problems from the perspective of Christian faith. His faith is based firmly on the simplicity and compassion of Jesus. It enables him to share with you his understanding of many current issues – family problems, alcoholism, suicide, emigration, the loss of faith, etc.

In the early chapters of this book the author writes movingly of his own upbringing, and of the parents and family who shaped his faith by example and love.

Price: £4.95

A LITTLE BIT OF RELIGION
by Father Brian D'Arcy, C.P.

We are pleased to make available again Father D'Arcy's first book, which has been out of print for some years.

The author writes – too modestly! – in his Introduction: "I know I'm not a skilled writer. But there are some honest thoughts expressed in the simplest and clearest way I know how. If you get a glimpse of a caring, loving, merciful, forgiving God, then it will have been worthwhile. Nothing else matters much." **Price: IR£5.95**

ORDER FORM

PLEASE SEND ME THE FOLLOWING BOOKS:

No. of Copies

· · · · · · **JUST A MOMENT** **(£4.95)**

· · · · · · **A LITTLE BIT OF RELIGION** **(£5.95)**

Please Include 60p per book to cover P/P
I enclose cheque / Postal Order / Money Order value £

Name . . . .

Address . . . .

. . . . .Phone. . . . .

Post to: CAMPUS PUBLISHING, 26 TIRELLAN HEIGHTS, GALWAY